# NEVER & ALWAYS

SHAHEEN ASBAGH

authorHOUSE®

AuthorHouse™
1663 Liberty Drive
Bloomington, IN 47403
www.authorhouse.com
Phone: 1 (800) 839-8640

Published by AuthorHouse   07/19/2016

ISBN: 978-1-5246-1932-9 (sc)
ISBN: 978-1-5246-1931-2 (e)

# CONTENTS

Visitation ....................................................................... 1
Adam and Eve ............................................................... 3
The Vail........................................................................... 8
The Adventures of the Greedy.................................... 11
Attention! ...................................................................... 13
Can we meet again? .................................................... 17
Sewer and Smoke ........................................................ 20
Pinball............................................................................ 23
The Chill ........................................................................ 26
Ode................................................................................. 28
In the Yard .................................................................... 30
Rainbow.......................................................................... 32
Olé .................................................................................. 35
Home .............................................................................. 37
Shy .................................................................................. 40
Acreage .......................................................................... 42
At The Front................................................................... 45
The Calm Before. . ....................................................... 47
House Of The Blues ..................................................... 50
D's Done ........................................................................ 53
Canyon ........................................................................... 56
An Ode To Peace .......................................................... 59
The Particles Of A Familiar Dust ................................ 62
Living Life By Those Hives .......................................... 65
Streaming The Truth Behind A Monitor...................... 68
The Adventure Of a knowledgable Sod ..................... 71
The Flight........................................................................ 74
Renegade's Vows Of Wrath .........................................77

As If It's The End Of The World ...............................................80

The Dance Of The Sands And Ice...........................................83

The Life Of A Manhood ........................................................86

Paris ................................................................................89

Homeless Are Coming!! ........................................................94

A Grain Of Light On Patriotism ..............................................97

Too High To Know Where .....................................................100

The Brief Life Of Sand And Sea ............................................103

A Socialist Friend Of Mine ...................................................106

Foam ...............................................................................109

Billy Joe's Promised Farm ...................................................112

We Will Love.......................................................................115

May Be It Is A Joke..............................................................118

Headlines Are Coming Easy ................................................121

The Promised Moment Of Love............................................124

So The Deed Is Done At Last...............................................127

2100s ...............................................................................129

Teach It!............................................................................131

Speak From The Dirt .........................................................134

Always And Never .............................................................137

With Utmost Confidence In Me Or You....................................140

Will Pray............................................................................143

My Crib .............................................................................146

A Song..............................................................................148

The Thrill...........................................................................150

Lost Memories ..................................................................154

Eternal Passage Of Gas .....................................................157

Growing Bones ..................................................................160

The Last Residence Of AKA: Dr. Hoodlum..............................162

Deemed Unjust..................................................................167

Well Paid And Independent .................................................170

An Ode To A Sentimental Bondage.......................................173

Time Is Also Measured........................................................175

# VISITATION

*That teardrop which adorns a candle*

*An empty cup that reads like a palm, a fate*

*The shady tree that shelters my wet skin*

*Those chirping birds of a feather that crowd the yard*

*The bouquet that warms a heart with love*

*These notions of truth that would come to a surface*

*When finally a few tender wrinkles redrew her face*

# Adam and Eve

*A child of elements, savvy and aware*

*At the underworld where sea provokes him to prepare*

*And stay along the waves of a natural wrath*

*He finds his north through this path*

*To leave of sand and trees behind*

*Searching like fish but not find*

*Wary and lost he begs mercy and retreat*

*Confessing time and time, praying without a treat*

*Truth has become an unknown in his religion*

*What is this which men praise and worship as a legion*

*It is this pulse more vivid than the site of light*

That never comes to him as much as a delight

Thus as the dirt under feels colder

The child's temper grows and becomes bolder

In the dark by the fire in the silence of the camp

A dream hits him like the magic lamp

He listens to that voice through the woods

He sees a few angels with hoods

He opens his sleepy eyes

As the sun in time fills the skies

He reaches for a tree

Bearing the fruit that sets him free

Holding his breath he thinks of his dream

There must be some truth to it, it seems

Drops of rain begin to feel the terrain

When the child begins to refrain

There was a hidden message last night

As he still struggled to find it wrong or right

Now it was different as the day broke

*Nature was now one with him and fire was smoke*

*The wind was blowing through the wild*

*As the sun still has not smiled*

*The sea he had found, it pretended in return*

*To assemble creatures that swam, tossed, and turned*

*Trees sat near the sand by the sea*

*trembling and setting his soul free*

*He raised his hands to the sky*

*"Help me survive and don't tell me a lie"*

*Then he saw his dream*


*It was all the same theme*

*He fell sunken in nature, thus his nature*

*Then sea brings a near glittering fixture*

*The boy now a man gets closer over the sand*

*Oh Lord. am I right? Is it answered, my demand!?*

*The shiny boat is covered with light*

*Shaheen Asbagh*

*That salty seawater innocent and bright*

*The horizon reflected a shadow of proportions*

*Approaching the boy in desirable motions*

*Suddenly our boy becomes alert and feels*

*As the bringing of the sea kneels*

*Reaching for her he is peeking*

*"Lord this is all that I was seeking!"*

*Shaheen Asbagh*

# THE VAIL

*In the spirit of loss the gavel brushes the wood*

*Ending the dispute in an unending amount that wrote*

*Us or them neither had the chance to vote*

*It was placed formally in lieu of the facts in the mood*


*The day that efforts subsided through good and bad*

*Prayers for a margin and hopes for a good wage*

*The room burst into jingles and the defense in rage*

*While the decision was mad*


*A call for order, a summon prepared by law*

*The decision is now final without a flaw*

# THE ADVENTURES OF THE GREEDY

*Placing time as a toy that plays with distance*

*Considering all or non, reconsider anything like resistance*

*Noting that which plays the role of time and money*

*Counting the specks of gold dug out just like milk and honey*

*Going to distance would I mean reaching a treasure*

*Pressing the pedal would ever bring yet any pleasure*

*Having reached all diggers with a good pitch*

*Presuming that is why now you are popular and rich*

# ATTENTION!

*Fallen halfway through this road*

*I now look back and instead of condescension there I
beseech forgiveness*

*Blessing our generation and how I see a place for
fathers and mothers*

*As every fact comes in a pair*

*How good, how bad*

*How late, how soon*

*What we had*

*What we're waiting for*

*Future is also colorful as it is*

*To prevail the past and even the score*

*Some of us will*

*Some of them wont*

*Some of us learn*

*Some of them lost*

*Behind the mask lies a new man*

*He is no blood of mine, he would kill at no cost*

*Some of us care*

*Some of them don't*

*Most of us know*

*And they don't dare*

*Because facing the truth drags the torso of humanity forward*

*As for them it's all stand and stare*

*How we can love*

*How they can hate*

*How the peace*

*How the war*

*If that is that*

*All is all*

*A call is a call*

*It all is not too far*

# CAN WE MEET AGAIN?

*Finding truth around you begins to look like a lie*

*When next to you and others*

*Are your kind in disguise, evil or good, and you're in no mood*

*Check it out*

*The other day we thought of you and your voice*

*If there was any truth to it we couldn't tell no more*

*Making a wish we thought it was time for a word*

*But it is hard these days to become one with one's self*

*So much noise, so much poise*

*How can we love one another*

*Or for old times' sake*

*See things like we want to at will*

*Unlike what they tell us there is something hidden*

*A contemporary home*

*A place for everyone*

*A world we need to fix*

# SEWER AND SMOKE

*Consensus beholds the groove man had and*

*Ain't got nothin' against what you say or play*

*Times are different and why I reject the word*

*Because it is bad and one never knows*

*If he is set to revive or survive*

*But experimentation is not always sad*

*When heavy air blows through the eternal ventilation*

*imposing special team meditation*

*I would say you're alright lad*

*And gas fills our hallucinations that a mask can not prevent*

*The issues mental or else*

*That chaos had us mad*

# PINBALL

*Let's top the madness*

*Man if I could alone*

*Stop the sadness*


*Down one nine to go*

*Where there is hate*

*This life goes slow*


*Play the machine*

*With power that is*

*All out but yet in*

*Shaheen Asbagh*

*What's in that I don't*

*ever with my soul*

*Say about what I won't*

*Keep in what I never*

*let out around*

*guys who are clever*

*The ultimate secret*

*In the hood, on the road*

*Is the song of regret*

*Lets contain this sadness*

*While body count says else*

*Let's stop this madness*

# THE CHILL

*Hammer banner raising noise lately*

*Our homies call it a noise or air*

*Our norms play it like a game of hopscotch around the shelters*

*While the sirens sound different everywhere*

*Ask me how many colors in picturing a fact*

*This art is ever a prey*

*And the target is exact*

*Ours does three*

*Those I know set thee free*

*Shaheen Asbagh*

# ODE

*Hope surrenders*

*With greetings afar*

*And beyond soul*

*And the heart of a white blossom*

*Remains secretly foul*

*In existence there are only a few words*

*One might say*

*Before and after*

*The carnal games people play*

# In the Yard

*Let find me near and allow this last statement*

*Through white and black, alas, good and bad*

*That don't read eye to eye*

*Without a hunch or a tie*

*Leave me free as I have told you, like the truth*

*Me and you are all that is here in the universe*

*Waiting our time to destiny as lovers in reverse*

# Rainbow

*Hail to freedom and Huck Finn's pride in the woods*

*Looking up to the sky we join hands remembering moods*

*Those that saved us as we lasted*

*Through war and abyss that cast it*

*Fortune tellers crowded the plains back and forth*

*People sought peace and hailed all sorts*

*Like hooves the lories revved up*

*And the treasure was hidden on the hilltop*

*Behold, the universe joins hands for once, for all*

*They all fancy a new world standing tall*

*Who would have known that the horizon set*

*In purple, yellow, pink*

*So glorious how those all met!*

# OLÉ

*The hat reminds him of the bull*

*The suit calls him a legend*

*The cape is his life's rhapsody*

*The crowd awaits a revenge, Olé*

*Beast or man!*

*Man or beast!*

# HOME

*Was it so strange to tap your feet*

*Smoothing out the corners of the aged family album*

*Praising what they left behind*

*What they shared*

*What they would do if they had been you*

*The images might burst into chaos or indeed*

*That gracefulness has always flowed in the veins of all*

*They knew or not*


*They lived their lives individually*

*And pride*

*Shaheen Asbagh*

*Perhaps these pictures will one day become a long tale*

*And from there, it goes on*

*Let us stay and not delay*

*Pave the way*

*And love without a say*

# SHY

*Story goes as tumbling Sam hides his shy within inseams*

*Friends tell him other than he has seen in his dreams*

*Better late! Sam finds his way through the tunnel of love*

*Safe now! He waits for the right time, to hunt his dove*

*Putting his money where for years to come*

*He could say proudly*

*It takes all that you could give*

*To shout 'love' loudly*

# ACREAGE

*Drops of water behold the peace!*

*Declared in between the horizontal vegetation*

*Taking the oath that season has begun*

*And straw hats will once again crowd the fields*

*To yet begin their battle against remoteness*

*Surviving days and days of the blazing rays of sun*

*And at the end they could at once whisper fairy tales*

*To their young ones*

*Those who are not counted*

*And others who are not wanted*

*The screeching door carries an enticing flavor*

*It seeps all over*

*The abundant crop that will be food*

*As well as the silent heritage covering*

*Acres and acres of reality*

*That which some body will take care of.*

# AT THE FRONT

*As my ration allowed for a brother*

*To share and pass without a bother*


*Our land would vouch for both of us*

*High and low, young and brave, that was most of us*


*The landscape was promising and green*

*Men! Proud, armed, and eyes keen*


*My home should be at peace now*

*I am still thankful, yet alive, and I don't know how*

# THE CALM BEFORE. . .

*The horizon seemed apart from the momentary sentiments*

*Common among those hours of the lost and final dusk*

*Soon moon would reveal its not so tender tusk*

*Half hidden behind the clouds*

*Lost lovers and melancholies, drawn in passion and rye*

*Never understanding that emotion indigenous*

*To pure observation and*

*Pursuing their selfish romance*

*Human greed is awaiting a late dawn as the cold*

*Lays its suspicious cape upon the exhausted foliage*

Shaheen Asbagh

*It is all performance*

*Yet it is agreed once the sweat subsides*

*And temples feel cool and calm*

*The storm is near, it is an intimate part of a cycle*

*It will show outside inside a room*

*Storm always talks the noblest words*

*To wash away any doubt*

*A near death situation*

*In or out. . . .*

Shaheen Asbagh

# HOUSE OF THE BLUES

*Dust appeared in fancied portions, it was afternoon*

*House was dark with light only willing to blink in the corners*

*As the familiar windows still showed my companion half-moon*

*Still before the heart of the night one hears mourners*

*One day begins to swear her last vows before the dawn*

*The foreign chills of the early winter scare the blossoms*

*Floor is icy and the flesh struggles to bring heat*

*Somewhere afar I hear a praise that fills every room*

*Love lost, and the cost of letting out moans of relief*

*Turn the edges and pave my zealous instincts leaf by leaf*

*Pondering the flaws of a house so quiet*

*My mind resists against it as if a riot*

# D's Done

*By the wall a man did his business*

*Listen!*

*He wrote his word as though listless*

*At the end of his devalued life*

*The graffitis reflected the sound and*

*The word on the street is rage*

*Why didn't they let the brother live. . .*

*Beware!*

*Justice is blind*

*It's for all*

*Dude was shivering in the cold*

*And the wording was flawed*

*Those words written in bold*

*Kids now understand likes of him*

*Pain in the crib and pain out*

*He was free doin' his business*

*He wasn't afraid*

*Either of being killed or being caught!*

# CANYON

*The circles stayed apart from the ground*

*Yet below the roof*

*As a herd of horses kept ashore*

*yet getting wet their hooves*

*To find a destiny, alas, look then!*

*You meant I was there deciding when*

*Running with them and*

*always beside was a friend*

*Forgot the name and my promise*

*seemed to bend*

*Hold my hand!*

*Instead my friend would say*

*Leave your misery. . . to live it*

*Today you may*

# An Ode To Peace

*Let us forget the past*

*That life, cruel and fast*

*Let us share what we mean*

*All there is, heard and seen*

*Let us begin to laugh*

*At the old man holding a staff*

*Let us teach one another*

*Like sister to sister, brother to brother*

*Let us escape our fears*

*Rejuvenate in laughter and tears*

*Shaheen Asbagh*

*Let us bring joy*

*Let us bring hope*

*Let us not destroy*

*Let us obey and cope*

# THE PARTICLES OF A FAMILIAR DUST

*Life is a dime worth a quarter*

*Used to be anything, everything, or getting smarter*

*Children grew through elementary and high school*

*Some made efforts, while elders were not so cruel*

*Now, the domino, turning tables and men*

*Who don't know no honest reason, their hands caved in*

*Elbow rubbing and a myriad of actions*

*Direct all to the end of such destined factions*

*Comes now the final stage of occupation*

*To detention, to perversion, and a near elation*

# LIVING LIFE BY THOSE HIVES

*My promises to our colony*

*Of bees in grief or harmony*

*And with pleasure, making a vow*

*That to please someone, time is now*


*When tenderness without proving*

*beguiles the soul, alive and moving*

*It seeps through colony's hives*

*Those I could touch with both fives*


*Thus selling a drop of honey*

*Wouldst be love and no money*

*Lasting longer than the taste of sin*

*Working one from within*


*That love and the forbidden resolution*

*Are all, by God, part of thy eternal evolution*

# STREAMING THE TRUTH BEHIND A MONITOR

*I-Mad, I-Sad, and numbers of icons that remind me of inner circuits*

*Plain lights that shine on those naughty pursuits*

*Load me with three apps that will cheer, energize, and revive me*

*My salty lips, and sweaty cheeks now easy to see*

*The haunted plenty that never stops*

*I and us think it as the season's crops*

*But the ease of sharing the truth and saving my passions in a file*

*Beats me every time I get up and stand on this intelligent tile*

*I tell the tale of daybreaks when I'm on my pad*

*My delusions, oh bring me a hope, driving me mad*

*I can, oh I can again*

*Withdraw and delete pain*

*And all that knocks me off my feet*

*Will I live through the new beat*

# THE ADVENTURE OF A KNOWLEDGABLE SOD

*Among a number of halfway friends*

*Finding ways of affection*

*With a million of touches*

*Unspoken but felt*

*Reviving those blessings we were once wished*

*And solace in the grass*

*Without those callous hopes*

*Of thee I spoke once*

*Thus, this lapse was revoked*

*In plain focus of senses*

*Shaheen Asbagh*

*It was man who was distinguished*

*With the sound of literacy*

*And poverty of knowledge*

*That he so desires*

*Shaheen Asbagh*

# THE FLIGHT

*Crazy how the blossoms bloom*

*Into maturity without fear or worry*

*Let it be known that nature is turbulent*

*Out of space and ubiquitous to contain life*

*There they fly and from one end to another*

*Sound reaches the darkest corner of the jungles*

*Without blooms the birds don't seem in air*

*Merely members of a flock in desperate passage*


*And without birds man would again face a wall*

*Of infinite destitute playing the tune of another age*

# RENEGADE'S VOWS OF WRATH

*Fight, all you all*

*Bang your fists*

*Let the air out*

*Rise! All you all!*


*Good people don't know*

*They want you*

*He wants you*

*Hell. . . all you all*


*There is a call you all*

*We won't have to*

*Shaheen Asbagh*

*Yank and shove*

*Take it! All you all*


*Stay put all you all*

*Let her fly*

*The promise of the land*

*Let's rise to the call. . . . all of you!*

*Shaheen Asbagh*

# As If It's The End Of The World

*Chieftain counts the lashes of the heat*

*That which is unlikely if the forces retreat*


*Battle never stops the pulse of a mass*

*The votes and unity always come last*


*To play the pawns like a wise lad*

*We must count on a cutting pen and a pad*


*The imperatives of a safe and sound border*

*Let us perceive a keen and loyal sorter*

*Troops are taught that very dedication*

*A sick man always has for his medication*

*Then a winner takes on the battlefield*

*Looser surrenders and barters his shield*

*Thus, we are all free and stricken with rage*

*'What was this infamy to which history dedicated a page?'*

# THE DANCE OF THE SANDS AND ICE

Helping the sands that hover over the promiscuous winds

Completes the chaos from the storms as it rescinds


Believe it wise to save time and help live this life

As skin resists the soft touch season where ice cuts like a knife


Cherry blossom too far away and summer farther back

The mountains are white and avalanche on the attack


Take a spin around to see how color paints this heaven

*Shaheen Asbagh*

*Skies are blue and shared by sparrow, dove, and raven*


*The short passed draught meant every drop counted*

*Now, the rivers are flowing and every boat is mounted*


*Counting the days to spring begins to look like a story*

*This misty season must be cherished for its icy glory*

*Shaheen Asbagh*

# THE LIFE OF A MANHOOD

*Strands of grass wave salutes to us*

*At the cost of being a loss and they fuss*


*The rivers talk new and old*

*Describing the tale of nature twofold*


*Trees are growing leaves and leaves are green*

*The celebration, again and again, all has been seen*


*Those peaks always cold and white*

*The wolves dance and the rams fight*


*My house yet has a comfort ever to be shared*

*And we are seldom apart like the wind and the stream paired*


*The sound of the echoes turn as thunder*

*The face of manhood becomes a wonder*

# PARIS

*Buried under the lights was the night*

*The noise and sentiments at their height*

*Streets blossoming quietly yet cars made the sound*

*Cherry lips and generous tips; couples on the mound*

*Afternoon had guided this darkness into its peak*

*Lovers breathlessly playing the hide and seek*

*It is known that this city has its own power*

*Where lights again adorn the Eiffel Tower*

*They say it was once brought in by parts*

*Shaheen Asbagh*

*Like all the strangers who had left their hearts*

*A plea of humanity always sides with this town*

*Like that after the war when hands were down*

*And peace echoes through Champs-Elysees in a stream*

*When guns rattled; a show done by a team*

*Why one time we are all the same and human*

*Another time we cannot stop or share the same pan*

*What shook the windows and doors cost many lives*

*The peace, goodness, and silence splinter and turn into jives*

*Screaming, suffocated, and running away*

*Is this the city of lights or somewhere you can't say?*

*Lives lost that no one would've ever believed*

*Men in madness and tension; messages sent and received*

*It is strange that they were welcome into the landmarks*

*Into the cafes, theaters, cabarets, and parks*

*Perhaps it was among friends, neighbors, or other klans*

*Having spent all that time creating their evil plans*

*If you want to shake heaven and don't know how*

*Dedicate yourself to reason and obey with a bow*

*Yet no! Humanity must be yet retrieving no facts*

*It is not reason not to seal crisis through pacts*

*As people suffer and guns heard*

*Peace is first, freedom second, and children third*

*There is a price for each man and woman lost*

*Shaheen Asbagh*

*Who are they whom upon we shall blame the cost*

*That day is a day in the life of all*

*Indeed news burst into chaos and defenders stood tall*

*Thus, the world should know that the truth*

*Yet lies remote without a logical proof*

*Shaheen Asbagh*

# HOMELESS ARE COMING!!

*I left home by force*

*Eventhough that day took its course*


*Found me a dark park*

*Dogs are lost and no bark*


*No one to be seen*

*My eyes worried yet keen*


*Daylight hazy close to noon*

*Desperate! I'd be hungry soon*


*I tried to leave no trace*

*But knew I had to find a place*

*Night had fallen too soon*

*Ever lonelier this bright moon*

*I come to rest at last*

*Felt my existence as an outcast*

*Will morning be any brighter*

*The burden of loss, lighter*

*I felt I no more belonged*

*Home, family, friends, so long!*

# A GRAIN OF LIGHT
# ON PATRIOTISM

*Leave your defenseless shack and prevail in the field*

*Hold your breath, feel your pulse! Pride being your shield,*

*Step forward, feel the soil; territory needs volunteers*

*And don't give up the freedom; be among the pioneers*

*Let the shady trees hide your wounds and all*

*Let the plains expand in directions and subvert this wall*

*A man's tale began in simple phrases*

*Nourishing him with truth, dignity, and respect*

*Now he is among family and children he raises*

*They need truth, dignity, and other aspects*

*Shaheen Asbagh*

# Too High To Know Where

*Blasphemy, as ubiquitous as death on a given hour*

*The distance between the minutes reflected in the wine
now sour*


*My vision dark and my ears so numb from the truth,
through a day*

*The week was going to end at the belly of a lamb in
the hay*


*My head trashed with moments, isolated, per say,
escaping doom*

*When truth be told; those flaws will bleed me soon*


*They had the youth and many days more vivid than the
ebbs of the sea*

*Others denied the chaste, pure, pallid instance having set us free*


*I could now merely breath and take steps away from the town*

*Over the mountain top, afar from streams that ever witnessed me looking down*

# THE BRIEF LIFE OF SAND AND SEA

*Waves are forever greeting the white sand*

*Sea eliminates its living just like a hired hand*


*Pleasant is the moment when they flee the water*

*Taking in the harshness of the hot sun with no bother*


*It is on land where they face the truth*

*Among species they search food and what may sooth*


*Day becomes the cycle through darkness and light*

*Among them, for relief, these creatures fight*

*Shaheen Asbagh*

*Survival tracing their path tree by tree*

*As theirs are a legend coming from the sea*

*A few die, and others pursue death still*

*Peace hardly seems like the sea that fills*

*Their lives with distinction and flow*

*Instead they end up not at the top of the hill but below*

*Such indigenous recognize the outsiders well*

*Feeding themselves with them cell by cell*

*Awaiting eternal pride on the ground or top of a tree*

*Scavenging and hoping for another taken out of the sea*

Shaheen Asbagh

# A Socialist Friend Of Mine

Partial loss of pride like the days of doom

My share of Eden has flown as I find hard to assume


Only one would survive the waves of hostile acts

That have painted my society apart from legitimate facts


The time would be up and you are standing

As welfare lines and shelter trays make life demanding


Those who know the child of freedom left in their jets

And others stayed silent suffering the tight duty nets


We do pay dues now, yes,. . . . we have done before

*Bowls of corrosion, life of emotion; all we could afford*

*Everyday end seems closer though neglected*

*This bamboozle spins, and still dances like those elected*

*We won't ever point at each other*

*Carrying the pain is no more a bother*

# FOAM

*Pull the plug on humanity*

*And then you are left with rage*

*Crisis everywhere, seeds of profanity*

*The news are written in red page by page*


*Let love lose its grip on you*

*And then hatred would bathe you in rage*

*You and them would have to pretend too*

*The news are written in red page by page*


*The playground now crowded by children everyday*

*Shaheen Asbagh*

*From sunup to sundown as they know it as home*

*It is to turn as memory through a play*

*These lovers are on that carousel made of foam*

*Shaheen Asbagh*

# BILLY JOE'S PROMISED FARM

*Witness in a good man*

*It is the fairy tale that becomes the truth*

*When it is revealed who can*

*Deny the fact that all has been proven and forsaken*

*As truth from a witness*

*reveals the purpose of a cell*


*We could not deny the affection*

*In the days and nights, through up and down*

*For others. . . . never mind the heat*

*And solely anticipating a reflection*

*Absence of blood and a broken heart*

*Showed the red dots to be a shade*

*When dusk settled around us*

*And the farmers carried the carts*


*Between us and the mood was one*

*Of golden hours and glamorous vows*

*Even wine had abandoned the race*


*In the escape from love in the sun*

# WE WILL LOVE

*Love turns around*

*Lost or found*

*Love carries a torch*

*Shines on a porch*

*Love joins hands*

*As far as distant lands*

*Love calms the soul*

*Becomes holy like a mole*

*Love knows the way*

*To happiness and constant play*

*Love that I love*

*Shaheen Asbagh*

*Love that you love*

*Love that we love*

*Love that they love*

# MAY BE IT IS A JOKE

*Speed up*

*How you always finish the line*

*Saying the last words to everything*

*Every story, every complain, every joke*

*Like the other day*

*'Really I'm fine!'*

*And I'm waiting*

*For friends it's fine*

*For me, cope and dine*

*But the truth*

*Always lies in the last line*

# HEADLINES ARE COMING EASY

*Struggling to build my crib in the vicinity*

*Shootings surrounding the old divinity*

*Better had been recognized*

*As the bloody dude acted uncivilized*

*The police saw the flaw in pursuit*

*It was nasty how the holy men sued*

*The paper downed the bust*

*To all the feds, homies, it was lust*

*Some twenty years old*

*Dead and lying down in the cold*

*The buster turned into a big time gangster*

*Shaheen Asbagh*

*Holy Cross brought down by a prankster*

*Shown under the red, white, and blue*

*It could've been the feds, brothers, or you*

*Last day of mayhem come now*

*Grace is scarce, it was all knowhow*

*Shaheen Asbagh*

# THE PROMISED MOMENT OF LOVE

*Finding her overcome solace and perceiving her sad separation*

*As wind catches the promiscuous leaves that adorn the ground*

*It's a usual autumn's tale in the memory of lost lovers in jubilation*

*I couldn't read her impression which cost me that bad habit of staying with sound*

*Rustling nature, chatters and whispers of birds was what covered her immensity*

*Yet soon they found a corner to settle; and wine and bread appeared*

*Let them rejuvenate in the woods without honesty*

*That which is revealed soon*

*Then the drama falls on the treetops; the only burden they feel as they peer*

*The light still played hide and seek, alas, she became a phase*

*In a remoteness that lasted willingly with a pulsing trace*

# So The Deed Is Done At Last

It is the far horizon of hope that does it

Leaving me behind its crashing wheels and its sound

Timidly convincing me that many tokens it places in a cradle

Would survive the vision which might leave a gypsy flawless

Yet as the bones exclaim the last vow of doom through witchcraft

Letting hardship, that burden of natural rhapsodic colors

Confide in all of us, old and new, far and new

As the zodiac summons Mercury and Pluto on its Milky Way day

# 2100s

*Vengeance fills the drops of sand*

*As men culminate into immortal vigilantes*

*Encompassing these morbids of the plain*

*Silence, still the falling character of the anthem*

*Draws near an impulse*

*That one which orbits the wind and terminates*

*What history constantly names*

# TEACH IT!

*After all, there are tokens of doom that*

*Rid of the sole morbid drops of solace*

*Forever young, the immortality allows the race*

*Bracing the wings of the timid falcon which sat*

*On the fortress of such castle as the heart and soul*

*Heights of emotion and loyalty in a capricious range*

*Could the last of them surmount the foreseen*


*Dreams of vengeance, spirit of loss among men and fowl*

*Be it the fate of the wondering renegades of love*

*Shaheen Asbagh*

*Still holding their gaze as they free the doves*

*To bring the words of the prophets*

*And flying high beyond that no soul could top*

*Shaheen Asbagh*

# SPEAK FROM THE DIRT

*I am gone*

*After I am gone*

*When death takes its place*

*Thereafter, over and done*

*The soul, my soul or a ghost*

*An unidentified image of the culprit*

*Which plays the aftermath host*

*The darkness that falls after the rays of light*

*They never fight*

*One like the rest*

*The rest of beings mortal or other*

*If remembered best*

*Now I'm human*

*A good human*

*It is said enough*

*Savvy and tough*

*Sunken in dirt*

*Pleading mercy*


*Curtailed on her epitaph*

# ALWAYS AND NEVER

*I see a moon*

*An eclipse so natural as I zoom*

*That's when I go*

*Oh! Your soft skin*

*The cloudy white*

*Adorned with tin*

*Baby you're out o' sight*

*You take your steps*

*Short, soft, and long*

*All that scent and preps*

*Puts me wordless in a song*

*Shaheen Asbagh*

*The peaceful waves of hair*

*Gives me no choice but stare*

*How can this feeling*

*A tender touch of bondage*

*Once felt, called stealing*

*Be a keeper as an advantage*

*Rescue me from an unheard ill*


*As your hiddens, still*

*Will you show me a way*

*I will listen to all you say*

*That secret hidden within your bosom*

*That scent keeping me all day*

*Like spring and its blossoms*

*Teach your way*

*And how we play*

Shaheen Asbagh

# WITH UTMOST CONFIDENCE IN ME OR YOU

*What I say to your sons and daughters*

*Believe it to be the sound of street*

*Half in, half out, like a half beat*

*Left alone inside the pipe and water*


*Letting out the cry*

*that puts ahead of all*

*That rule we abide*

*Through every call*

*The civilized let the city try*

*Be one with God*

*As us with divinity*

*Find one reason my good friend*

*This I mean it as though it's odd*


*Your due respect*

*Stay aside*

*All that we got and what's missed*

*It is not a lie*


*Facts are in*

*Don't press your luck*

*Get on the ride*

# WILL PRAY

*They thought they made it*

*Pain to tenderness and loss to love*

*Come! Let it fall deep in haze*

*They thought they made it*

*Running far to the shooting stars*

*They waited to see the miracle*

*Come! It's all far and then to stay*

*The night ended the solar for lunar*

*Raising their hands to the clouds*

*Begging the silence of the galaxy*

*Covering the soft and fluid sky*

*Shaheen Asbagh*

*To tell the tale of the lost crowds*

*It seemed they had to gather*

*Alas, up the plains, peacefully rather*

*Without vengeance or mercy*

*Without a call for fraud or heresy*

*Believing they would take it*

*They thought they made it*

# My Crib

*Let blood paint the hood while you're at it*

*The command will only rule humanity if served hot*

*There it is, the smoking gun along the flames*

*The burning pink caddy belonged to the bitch*

*Watching them bitches on those high toes*

*Letting them lend an ear to the popping noise*

*The truth being in as true life among lives*

*Our streets crowded of sorts with no dead ends*

*The society filled with dust and lead still broadens*

# A Song

*As the singer retains*

*A rhythm akin only to a drummer*

*Lifeless breaths begin to surround*

*her rhetoric physical presence*

*The harmony will disappear*

*Everyone knows*

*What the crowd is now left with*

*Are the strings, pipes, and hide*

*Shaheen Asbagh*

# THE THRILL

*Strands of hay bent like an arrow*

*Aiming at the heart of nature*

*Gleaming in the twilight*

*Like a prodigal fixture*


*When lovers share moments*

*And they add up to dawn*

*Alas, never thought that in this circus*

*There is a clown*


*The king of the wild stands*

*In silence yet quite mute*

*And nature only speaks*

*When love changes into feud*


*As the hay never blossoms*

*Unless sewing its seeds in the wind*

*The youth and the the heat of momentous actions*

*Will compose anew and continue to rescind*


*Pleasure would have a new name*

*And lovers a new game*

*This complete form of rhapsody*

*Gains a new fame*


*Soil like blood*

*Emotion as flood*

*A man plays a woman*

*The clock turns Roman*


*Passes the twilight*

*Shaheen Asbagh*

*And grips around the morning*

*As the sun plays*

*The lovers' skin like a warning*

# Lost Memories

*In rage, what was forgotten*

*Once again blended in the light,*

*The light in my life*

*The tremble of its rays*

*And forgotten was a poor word*

*And forgotten was the reflection*

*It, too, beheld my immense oblivion*

*Unable to name those things*

*The things in my life*

*The belongings even though human*

*So near and flawlessly luring*

*Always had brought me back*

*Shaping, preparing, and helping me remember*

# ETERNAL PASSAGE OF GAS

*Divine elements of*

*That piety called appetite*

*Free my soul*

*without a need to be upright*

*Holy favors that came*

*In lumps or loaves even*

*Extend the night into*

*An escapade called heaven*

*God save all at the table*

*A creation in an askance or a bow*

*Let my people free at last*

*Shaheen Asbagh*

*This gourmet is indeed without a flaw*

*Saints of last dinner along*

*With crusaders of desert and plain*

*Merely innocence tells this tail*

*Of fillet and potato on a flame*

*Angels of a holy spirit*

*Embody the aroma of dill*


*Hidden as the last testament*

*Between shanks on a burning grill*

*Lord save the night*

*Because tomorrow is far apart*

*In a breath of garlic might*

*Bless me if I had to fart*

# GROWING BONES

*Day one as we remember*

*Was like the child's December*

*Struggle for toys and candy*

*My own fate seeming handy*

*Facing age by the number*

*That was our November*

*Paper and cardboard piles*

*Setting a record in shapes and styles*

*We had the time of our times*

*Me and my child weary of the chimes*

*Shaheen Asbagh*

# THE LAST RESIDENCE OF AKA: DR. HOODLUM

*I wanna try telling you a tale*

*Making it short so the drama won't fail*

*I gotta touch you deep down*

*And promise to stop once you frown*

*A story that puts the kids to sleep*

*And elders to dig down deep*

*Talkin' about a home so warm*

*Food is plenty and humor swarms*

*The season at best and wind blowing west*

*Ma and Pa work hard then rest*

*The sound of music and laughter*

*Draw a picture of hereafter*

*Children amazed at the dog*

*Playing the ball under the rug*


*In the dusty summer a stranger knocks*

*A lazy and grey man but a tall jock*

*Helpless, he needed only food*

*His gesture strange, his tone rude*


*Pa lets him in, offers a seat*

*'Ma should come and soon you'll meet. .'*

*He placed his stash on the table*

*Browsing and thinking of a fable*

*Children gather and laugh*

*It was almost noon and a half*

*He eyes them with a pallid face*

*At once the kids step away and race*

*Shaheen Asbagh*

*Ma says she'll be a minute*

*Yells at the dog in the kitchen, 'beat it!'*


*That night pa tells ma 'I love you'*

*The stranger gets a dinner and a bed too*

*His one day stay turns into weeks*

*Ma asks him what in life he seeks*

*No home, no family, no job*

*The man explains holding a corn on the cob*

*The family places him in their hearts*

*Now working and helping for his part*

*Chopping logs, feeding the stock, or collecting eggs*


*Every day and night gives excuses and begs*

*His condition improves with time*

*But destiny and his plans don't rhyme*

*One night he pleads to God*

*He was worried and mad, the poor sod*


*One mornin' pa and ma are headed for town*

*They trust him with kids and tending the front lawn*

*House was quiet and the oven burning*

*The stranger napping, tossing and turning*

*The son comes in for a cookie*

*Now about fourteen and a rookie*

*The son raises the flame to warm up*

*Some milk and honey in a tin cup*

*Others shout his name,'come out son!'*

*He bites his cookie and forgets which on the run*

*Blaze was sudden and spreads fast*

*While children cried a shadow of smoke was cast*

*The stranger was to take the blame*

*He was dreaming and died in vain*

# DEEMED UNJUST

*I demand charity,*

*As my heart is still taken away*

*And left stray in a stream*

*Of memories that now and then fulfill*

*The lowest instincts while never suffering*

*I demand blessings,*

*To suit that divided mind which*

*Shaheen Asbagh*

*Pursues, always and ever, the unending*

*Beams of a departed intention*

*Leaving homeless that who sheltered*

*Shaheen Asbagh*

# WELL PAID AND INDEPENDENT

*I fly in my private jet and think of my hits, those*

*I would compose to serenade my fans*

*And my playmates for dates that*

*I would accompany in high fashion attending*

*A beach party in my resort, top fillet mignon and sauteed onions*

*All paid through my accounts while*

*I drive a fancy Tesla*

*And next to me my lies, my briefcase*

*All where it's at*

*A trick in the hat*

*Steaks*

*Albums*

*Playmates*

*Clothes*

*Resorts*

*Millions*

*Cars*

*Executive. . .*

# AN ODE
# TO A SENTIMENTAL BONDAGE

*Love comes when you call my name*

*Enduring your pain is my claim of fame*

*In this time of grace and joy*

*It's the season playing me like a toy*

# Time Is Also Measured

*I dig the shadow of war*

*Out of a jar*

*Post the blessings of mother*

*And don't bother*

*Searching for the truth, hear. . . .!?*

*With Easter near*

*Half frozen and other worries*

*I remember glories*

*And twilights of the liberty*

*When slave became celebrity*

*Common cause of proud and brave*

*Shaheen Asbagh*

*Sharing this home to save*

*I played my six cents best I could*

*But don't know if I would*

*Change my comforted mind*

*With devotion and bind*

*To compare us and that game*

*Of us earthlies in vain*


*Play where the blood*

*Poor man and stud*

*Running ahead breathless*

*Enemies devout but helpless*

*I yet cherish this chance*

*And defy a lack of balance*

Printed in the United States
By Bookmasters